How To Develop Your Reading Skill

Dr. Rhoda Martins

INTRODUCTION

CHAPTER ONE

READ FOR PLEASURE

CHAPTER TWO

SET GOALS

CHAPTER THREE

FIND A MENTOR

CHAPTER FOUR

USE TECHNOLOGY

CHAPTER FIVE

DON'T FORGET ABOUT AUDIO BOOKS

CHAPTER SIX

13 STEPS FORMULA TO IMPROVE YOUR READING SKILL

CONCLUSION

INTRODUCTION

How often do you read books? If you don't read much, then you should start now. Reading is a great way to improve your vocabulary and expand your knowledge base.

Reading is a very important part of life. It helps us to stay informed, gain new skills, and even enjoy ourselves.

If you want to become a good writer, you need to practice reading. Reading books and articles helps you gain knowledge and understanding.

To become a better reader, you should start by improving your vocabulary. Once you master the basics, you can move on to other aspects such as grammar and punctuation.

some people struggle to read well because they lack basic skills such as comprehension and fluency.

if you're having difficulty understanding what you read, you might benefit from help to develop reading skills.

reading aloud helps improve your ability to understand and grasp the meaning of a text.

If you have good reading skills, you will be able to make it to university or even college.

A great book is one that you love and enjoy reading, and it has a meaning and message that you want to pass on to others.

There are several ways to improve your reading skills. The key is to practice regularly. Try these simple steps to get started.

CHAPTER ONE

Read for pleasure

You can find many interesting books at the library or online. Read something that interests you. This will help you become more engaged with what you're reading.

How often do you pick up a book or magazine and wonder why you don't enjoy reading anymore? Reading is a great way to relax and unwind after a long day at work. But sometimes, books can be intimidating. How do you get started?

Reading is a skill that requires practice. If you want to improve your skills, start by picking up a good book. There are plenty of ways to go about it. For example, you can read fiction or nonfiction, depending on your preference.

You should also consider the type of book you want to read. Some books require a certain level of knowledge, whereas others are easier to follow. Here are some ideas to help you choose the perfect book.

1. Choose a Book Based on Your Interests

If you're looking for something fun to read, try a novel. A story is an excellent choice if you like to escape into another world. However, if you prefer more in-depth information, opt for a textbook. These types of books will teach you everything from history to math. You can even find them online!

2. Pick Up a Classic

If you love classic literature, there are many options available. Try one of these: The Adventures of Tom Sawyer, To Kill a Mockingbird, Frankenstein, Pride and Prejudice, or Great Expectations. They all have their own unique style and appeal.

3. Read What You Love

If you already know what you want to read, then just dive right in. It doesn't matter whether it's fiction or nonfiction; as long as you enjoy it, you'll keep coming back for more.

4. Start with Short Stories

Short stories are a great place to start because they give you a taste of what you'd expect from longer works. In addition, short stories are easy to digest. This means you won't feel overwhelmed when you begin reading.

5. Find Books Online

If you've always wanted to learn how to play guitar, but never had the time to take lessons, now might be the best time to start. Instead of going out to buy a book, you could simply search online. Many websites offer free resources to help you learn music theory.

6. Check Out Audiobooks

Audiobooks are a great option for people who struggle with learning new things. When listening to an audiobook, you only need to focus on the words and not worry about understanding the language. Plus, you can listen while doing other things, such as driving or working out.

7. Get Help From Friends

Sometimes, we just need someone else to tell us what to read next. Ask friends and family members for recommendations. Or, you may decide to join a book club.

8. Look At Reviews

Before buying a book, check reviews first. Readers usually share their opinions about different titles. If you see positive feedback, you'll likely enjoy the same thing.

9. Keep Reading

Once you've found a few books you'd like to read, make sure to continue exploring. Don't stop until you've read every single page.

10. Take Notes

When you finish a book, write down anything you liked or didn't understand. This way, you'll remember what you learned without having to reread the entire text.

11. Share Your Experience

When you're done reading, let your friends know by posting a review on Goodreads.com. Sharing your experience with others helps everyone improve their reading skills.

12. Make Time For Yourself

Reading isn't just for leisure anymore. There are so many benefits to reading that it's important to schedule some time each week.

13. Write Down Your Thoughts

After you've finished reading, don't forget to jot down any thoughts you have. Writing down your ideas allows you to organize your thoughts better.

14. Learn More About What You Enjoyed

If you enjoyed a certain book, take the time to look up more information about it. Learning more about something you love will bring even greater enjoyment.

15. Join A Book Club

Book clubs are a fun way to meet new people and discuss topics related to books. Most communities have at least one book club meeting per month.

CHAPTER TWO

Set goals

What would you like to accomplish by improving your reading skills? Do you want to learn how to write a better essay? Maybe you'd like to be able to understand more complex scientific concepts. Whatever it is, set some realistic goals.

How often should I read? How much time should I spend each day? What kind of books should I choose? These questions can be overwhelming, especially if you don't know where to start.

Reading is important for everyone, regardless of age or gender. Reading helps us develop our vocabulary, improve our memory, and increase our knowledge. If you want to become a better reader, then you need to set goals and stick to them.

Set a daily reading goal. Choose a book that interests you. Read every day. Don't make the mistake of choosing a book that you think you will like but end up hating. You will only get through it once, so it's best to find something you really enjoy.

Set a weekly reading goal. Choose one book you have been meaning to read. Or try picking out two different books from your favorite author. It doesn't matter how long they are – as long as you finish them both!

Try setting a monthly reading goal. Pick three books that interest you. One could be fiction, another non-fiction, and the last could be an anthology. The more variety in your selection, the more likely you are to actually complete all three.

If you feel overwhelmed by the idea of setting goals, then just pick one thing to do this month. For example, you could decide to read at least 20 pages per day (or 30 minutes) on Tuesday and Thursday evenings. That way, you won't feel guilty when you miss other days.

If you're struggling with reading motivation, then try these tips:

Read about what you love. This may sound obvious, but it's easy to lose sight of why we started reading in the first place. When you begin to read a book, ask yourself "Why am I here?"

Make sure you're getting enough sleep. Lack of sleep makes it harder to focus on tasks, including reading. Try going to bed earlier and waking up later.

Get rid of distractions. Turn off your phone, computer, TV, tablet, etc., before starting any task. Otherwise, you might not even remember to turn them back on after you've finished.

Take breaks. Sometimes, it's hard to keep focused on a single activity for too long. Take a short break every hour or so. Go outside and take a walk around the block. Listen to music while you work.

Reward yourself. Once you've completed a certain amount of reading, reward yourself with a small treat. Maybe it's a cupcake or ice cream cone. Whatever works for you.

Don't forget to share your progress with friends and family. They'll be impressed by your achievements, and you'll feel good knowing you're helping others learn new things.

Start with the end in mind

Think of all the things you'd like to accomplish with your reading, and then come up with steps you can take towards those goals. Your first step is choosing a book to read. Read a book that's relevant to your goals, and find other books that you'd like to read. You might start by reading books on the same subject as your goals, like scientific writing or essay writing.

Read, read, read

Don't just look at the list of books available in the library. You can find free online books, or borrow books from a friend. Reading helps you learn. If you want to learn how to write a better essay, try writing some notes about books you read. The more you read, the more you'll understand.

When you find a good book to read, read it. You'll find that reading for fun is more satisfying than just reading to try to learn something.

Read with a goal in mind

When you find a book you want to read, think about why you are reading. What are you hoping to get out of it? Be sure to write down any questions you have while you are reading, to help you remember.

Read in a different way

Reading is an active process. If you're reading to try to learn, you need to keep reading, and then reading some more. Reading isn't a spectator sport. You want to use your time efficiently, so if you find a book you'd like to read but don't have time to read it, try writing a list of questions you want to ask about it. It might help you decide what to do next time.

CHAPTER THREE

Find a mentor

How often do you read books or magazines? Reading is a great way to improve your vocabulary, expand your knowledge base, and even get some inspiration from other cultures.

There are lots of ways to enjoy reading, whether you prefer fiction or nonfiction. Some people love to curl up with a good book at night, while others prefer to read during their commute or while they exercise.

Reading is a great hobby, but sometimes it can become a chore. If you want to find a new passion, consider finding a reading mentor. This person can help you discover new genres, develop your skills, and even share their favorite reads with you.

Finding the right reading mentor for you may take time, so don't rush into things. Start by asking yourself these questions:

What kind of reader are you? Do you like to read alone or in groups? Are you more interested in fiction or non-fiction?

What kinds of books do you usually read? Is there anything that you avoid because it makes you uncomfortable?

Do you have any special interests when it comes to reading? For example, if you're particularly interested in history, what types of books would be most helpful for you?

Do you have friends who also enjoy reading? You could ask them about their favorite authors, which genres they like best, and how they go about selecting books.

If you'd rather not talk to anyone else about your reading preferences, you can always look online. There are plenty of websites where readers post reviews of different books. These sites include Goodreads, Amazon, LibraryThing, and BookLikes, just to name a few.

You might also want to join a book club. Many libraries offer free programs where you can meet other readers, discuss topics, and learn about new books. In addition, many book clubs will host events where members can meet and chat over drinks or snacks.

You can also find local book clubs through your library system. Your librarian should be able to point you toward resources that will help you start meeting other readers.

If you're looking for an older adult who enjoys reading, try joining a seniors group. These groups provide opportunities to socialize, as well as to exchange advice on everything from gardening to cooking. They can also give you tips on how to choose books that appeal to older adults.

When you've found someone who shares your interest in books, make sure to let them know! It's important to maintain a relationship with your mentor, especially if you plan to continue reading together. Don't forget to thank them for helping you grow as a reader, and tell them all about your latest discoveries.

The Benefits Of Having A Mentor

A mentor can be a valuable resource. Not only does he/she teach you new skills, but they can also introduce you to new ideas, experiences, and places.

A good mentor will encourage you to pursue your passions. He/she won't push you to follow a particular career path, but instead will show you how to turn your talents into a rewarding career.

A mentor can help you overcome obstacles. Whether you're struggling with schoolwork, dealing with family issues, or simply trying to figure out what you want to do with your life, having a mentor can be invaluable.

Having a mentor is one of the best ways to improve your writing skills. If you're serious about becoming a writer, you need to develop strong communication skills. The best way to achieve this goal is to practice writing every day. However, you may feel discouraged at times. When you encounter problems while writing, don't worry—your mentor can help you solve these problems.

Having a mentor helps you stay organized. As you get older, it becomes more difficult to keep track of things such as bills, appointments, and deadlines. But a mentor can act as a sounding board, providing feedback and encouragement so that you can remain focused.

Your mentor can help you build a network. This is particularly helpful when you're starting out. You can use your mentor to connect you with people who share your interests.

Your mentor can help you set goals. Sometimes we lose sight of our dreams because we become overwhelmed by the amount of work required to reach those goals. However, a mentor can help you identify realistic goals and then guide you towards achieving them.

Mentors are often willing to lend their time and expertise to others. That means you can ask your mentor to read your manuscript before you submit it to publishers. Or maybe your mentor can offer suggestions on how to market your novel. Whatever you need, your mentor can help you succeed.

CHAPTER FOUR

Use technology

There are so many tools available today that can help you improve your reading skills. For example, there are apps that allow you to highlight words as you read along. Or there are websites that provide vocabulary lists. These resources can really help you on your journey.

Technology has changed our lives in ways we couldn't imagine even five years ago. From smartphones to tablets, from computers to laptops, from smart watches to virtual reality headsets, technology has become part of our daily life.

There are many advantages of using technology in reading. For example, you can read books anywhere at anytime. Also, technology makes it easier to access information.

The most powerful resource of all technology to help with reading, is the Internet. You can search the web for websites about reading and English. There are many websites like that. One website is www.english.com. It is owned by the University of California. This website provides information and articles about English grammar and English as a second language. You will find there a lot of useful information for you.

The Internet, especially Google and Facebook, has also been used in the teaching of reading. In schools, the Internet is used by a large number of students to search for the answer to questions. Teachers post and organize their worksheets online.

For most people, the most difficult task is to read. There are many reasons why people do not enjoy reading. You can be too lazy to read or you might feel bored by reading certain books. You can also find it very difficult to understand a book. For some people reading can be a problem for them. They can't concentrate on reading. Some of these people may be diagnosed with dyslexia.

Top 10 Reading Tools

Here are the top ten reading tools that I personally recommend. These include ebooks, apps, websites and more.

The Kindle Paperwhite is a great ebook reader given away by Amazon in partnership with Scholastic. It offers a high level of usability and convenience for students who like to read on their own time.

The Kindle app is available for Android and iOS devices. You can download free sample chapters of many popular children's books as well as access your library collection.

The Kindle Fire HDX 7" tablet has an 8-inch display and is perfect for kids who love to read. It includes features such as parental controls, which allows parents to set up profiles for different users.

The Nook Simple Touch is another e-book reader that comes with a built-in browser. This means that you don't have to use any other apps to browse the web.

The Nook app is available for both Android and iOS devices. There are over 1 million digital titles available for the Nook.

The Kobo Glo is one of my favorite e-readers because it's easy to navigate and it looks good. It also has a backlight so you can read even if it's dark outside.

Kobo is a Canadian company based in Waterloo, Ontario. They offer a wide variety of books, including classics, non-fiction, fiction, manga and graphic novels.

The iPad is a great device for reading. The iBooks app lets you buy books online and download them directly to your device.

iPad owners can also connect their iPads to iTunes libraries and read books purchased through Apple's store.

The iPad Mini is a smaller version of the iPad. It's ideal for younger readers.

CHAPTER FIVE

Don't forget about audio books

Audiobooks are becoming increasingly popular because they offer a unique experience. They allow listeners to immerse themselves in stories without having to worry about missing out on anything important.

You don't have to worry about falling asleep or being interrupted by a phone call. Audiobooks also provide a great opportunity to listen to something new. And since they're read aloud, you can enjoy them even if you're driving or working out.

You can listen to an entire book in one sitting and still get all the benefits of reading it.

In fact, studies have shown that people who listen to audiobooks read more because it's a habit they've built from years of reading books on paper. And they'll usually read more books than they would if they were just listening to audiobooks.

If you need to relax after a long day at work, there's no better way to wind down than by listening to a book. And even if you don't listen to audiobooks, they're still a great idea. You could always grab a book and read it in your spare time.

So, the next time you're stuck in a long meeting at work, you can get yourself out of there in a productive way by turning on a book.

How to choose the right audio book

Whether you're trying to read a book for the first time or you want to listen to an audiobook again, you'll want to find the right one.

First, consider the type of book you want to read. Do you like to read short stories or you prefer to read novels? Do you prefer easy to read books or you'd rather delve into complex storylines?

Do you enjoy mysteries or you love reading science fiction? There are tons of genres and you'll find something you'll love.

Don't forget about the characters.

If you want to read about a hero, it's probably best to choose something action-packed.

If you enjoy stories with a lot of twists, maybe you want to pick up a thriller or a mystery.

If you're looking for a different experience, maybe you want to read about a heroine. But you can also enjoy stories about other characters.

If you're reading a book for the first time, you'll also want to consider the type of reading experience you want.

There are lots of different formats that you can use to get an audiobook read.

Some audiobooks will let you read along in your own pace. And you can even choose how fast to read.

If you want to read along as fast as you can, you can turn on fast-forward. You can also select the speed that you want to read at.

Some audiobooks offer multiple options.

These options let you choose how long the book will play for and how fast it will go.

You can also choose between listening and reading.

You can read along at the pace that you prefer. You can also read at the same speed as the author.

If you're doing audio recordings at home, you can read along at whatever pace you want.

You can also play it for short durations of time to see if you want to read a book more before buying it.

Listening to them while driving, exercising, or doing chores is a great way to keep focused and improve your listening comprehension.

CHAPTER SIX

13 Steps Formula to Improve your Reading Skill

There are several ways to improve your reading skills. The key is to choose the right method. Here are some tips to get you started.

1. Read Books – One of the best ways to improve your reading skill is by reading books. You can find many good books in bookstores or online. Choose one that interests you and start reading it. Don't worry if you don't understand everything. Just keep on reading until you finish it. This will help you learn more about the topic.

2. Watch TV Shows – Watching television shows is another great way to improve your reading skills because they usually contain lots of information. You can watch them while doing other things like cooking or cleaning. Or you can simply sit down and enjoy watching them.

3. Listen To Music – Listening to music while reading is an excellent way to improve your reading speed and comprehension. Try listening to different types of music such as classical, jazz, rock, etc. Find songs that have lyrics and try singing along with them.

4. Use Apps – Using apps to improve your reading skills is a great idea. Some of these apps include: Kindle, Google Play, iTunes, Audible, Amazon Prime, Netflix, etc. They all have their own advantages and disadvantages. So choose which one works for you.

5. Take Notes – Taking notes while reading is another effective way to improve your reading skill. Write down what you want to remember from each paragraph. Then go back and review those notes later.

6. Practice – As we mentioned before, practice makes perfect. So, make sure you practice whenever possible. Do this by practicing reading aloud. Also, try to answer questions related to the topics discussed in the text.

7. Ask Questions – When you read something, ask yourself questions about it. For example, when you read a story, ask yourself why the author wrote it. Why did he/she write it? What was his/her purpose? These are just some examples.

8. Keep Up with Current Events – Keeping up with current events is another great way to increase your reading skills. Read newspapers, magazines, blogs, etc. to get updates on what's happening around the world.

9. Join A Book Club – Joining a book club is a great way to meet people who share similar interests. They can be friends or relatives. But whatever the case may be, they will definitely be able to provide you with useful advice and feedback.

10. Be Active On Social Media – Being active on social media is another great way to enhance your reading skills. Posting comments on Facebook or Twitter about interesting articles will surely help you improve your reading skills.

11. Attend Meetings And Conferences – Attending meetings and conferences is another great way to expand your mind. You will be exposed to new ideas and concepts. This will help you become a better reader.

12. Learn Another Language – Learning another language is yet another great way to improve reading skills. If you know how to speak Spanish, French, German, Japanese, Chinese, Arabic, etc., then you should consider learning more languages.

13. Learn How to Code – Coding is another great way to learn how to improve your reading skills. It involves writing computer programs. There are many websites out there that offer free tutorials on coding. All you need to do is search online.

CONCLUSION

Reading is a very important part of life. It helps us to stay informed, gain new skills, and even enjoy ourselves. Whether you are a teacher or a student, you will always benefit from reading books as they bring a wealth of knowledge and a whole new experience. A book can take you away from your daily problems, allowing you to forget about them for a while, and can even teach you new things about life. If you are a passionate reader, you should definitely consider the tips provided in this book

www.ingramcontent.com/pod-product-compliance
Ingram Content Group UK Ltd.
Pitfield, Milton Keynes, MK11 3LW, UK
UKHW022008190726
13853UKWH00004B/1810

9 798424 103384